The more you ⌐_____⌐
nance, the more your decisions will be informed.

FINAL THOUGHTS

Tasha will continue to be the source of pride for her family as she embarks on a successful financial journey that will benefit her and her family.

NOTES

NOTES

NOTES

CHAPTER 2

Credit Card Management Including Budgeting/Net Worth Statement

When I was young, people lived paycheck to paycheck. Today, it seems like they live from credit card payment to credit card payment.

—Robert Kiyosaki

Credit card debt is at an all-time high. According to the Federal Reserve Bank of New York, American consumers have about $3.93 trillion of total issued card credit and have about $900 billion of credit card balances (3). This means the average American has about $12,000 in credit card debt, and many of these balances are at high interest rates with the average being 15 percent according to the Federal Reserve. Now, it is no wonder Americans are struggling to make ends meet and save when so much of their income goes toward credit card payments, with many making only minimum payments which can force individuals to take twenty years or more to pay off a credit card balance.

Let's meet Kim who is struggling with her finances, in particular credit card debt.

Forty-year-old, single Kim presented to my office for counseling. She has found herself in serious financial trouble; she was in significant debt. It was an insidious journey because she is unsure of how she got here. She admits she was much more financially responsible in her twenties; she had a great paying job, no student loans because she received a full scholarship to college, and she had no consumer debt such as a credit card. She never had a car note until her thirties because she would save her money to pay for her cars outright. In those early years, she hated the thought of a car note. She admits she was not a big saver because she loved to travel, eat out, and shop. But Kim managed to save a bit, approximately 5 percent of her income to her company's 401k account, and she had company matching. So, all was not lost. She doesn't remember when things got out of control, but she believed it started after she was laid off from her job and found herself out of work for eight months. She utilized credit cards to pay for living expenses including groceries, utilities, and other living expenses such as smartphone and car expenses such as maintenance. She also admits she is a spender and found herself buying unnecessary items at times to make her feel better, i.e., retail therapy. Because her budget was so tight, before she knew it, she was nearly $75,000 in credit card debt with no emergency fund to count on and with retirement within a twenty-five-year horizon. She felt lost and despondent and just did not know what to do.

DISCUSSION OF GOALS

Before we moved into the financial planning aspect of her visit, I had to work with Kim on her mindset. I dedicated one session to discussing her fears and the path that led her to this point. She was feeling pretty awful about her financial picture. We discussed ways and methods on what she could do to change her mindset. The tools that

I recommended included visualization and affirmations. Visualization is the act of picturing the reality you desire in your mind with the belief that whatever you imagine will result in actuality. I also recommended affirmations which are statements aimed to change the conscious and the subconscious mind, so that they in turn affect our behavior, thinking patterns, habits, and environment. She needed to understand that she can change her situation as along as she changes her behavior and does not beat herself up for past actions.

Now that she had a game plan for the right mindset, we discussed her goals. Her **short-term goal (within two years)** is to get out of debt. $75,000 is a great deal of debt especially under the time frame.

Long terms goals (beyond two years): Once she eliminates debt, she plans to establish an emergency fund and rev up her retirement savings since retirement is twenty-five years down the line.

I suggested she use the SMART acronym to guide the development of her goals.

S is for Specific. Kim stated she wants to be debt-free in two years. That is a great goal, but we need specifics. The questions she needs to answer are: How will she reduce such a large amount in such a short period of time? How much of her income will she devote to debt reduction? Does she have enough income to allocate toward debt reduction?

M stands for Measurable. How will Kim measure her goal? That is easy! She can use debt reduction calculators to monitor her achievements each month and she will also see a reduction in credit balances on her credit card statements.

A is for Attainable. This means, is this goal truly attainable? Meaning, is eliminating $75,000 worth of debt in two years something she could really do? Both Kim and I believe she can be aggressive in achieving this goal.

R stands for Realistic or Relevant. Kim believes this is realistic, achievable, and very relevant to achieving financial independence including having enough to retire, travel, leave something to her family, friends, and charities she cares about.

T is for Timely or Time-Bound. To track her goals, she needs to set target dates to review her achievements. She can monitor her progress monthly, quarterly or biannually. For example, she can review her credit card balances January 1, April 1 , July 1, and October 1 of each year.

STEPS

1st Step – Now that she has set goals, I advised Kim that we needed to get a complete understanding of where she stands now. I asked her to gather all of her financial documents because she needs to get an honest assessment. These documents include credit card statements, student loan statements, banking and investment statements, several months of utility bills, mortgage or rental statements, car notes, daycare or school expenses, home or rental insurance, car insurance, and groceries. I also suggested she download bank and/or credit card statements because many credit card statements or online programs will categorize expenses in certain categories such as transportation, housing, utilities, etc. This will assist her preparation. Next, we will be organizing her information. I suggested she purchase an accordion folder from Staples (or any home office store) and begin to categorize and file appropriately. You can also file information in an online folder program. Personally, I am old-school (and a former accountant), so I organize by downloading statements and using Microsoft Excel, but there are many online programs, such as QuickBooks, Mint, and Evernote that help with organization. Next, she compiles her paperwork (or online folders), and she will categorize and separate her expenses between fixed expenses and variable expenses. A fixed expense is an expense you incur on a regular basis, and the expense amount is essentially the same each period. Examples of fixed expenses would be your monthly mortgage or rental payment, your car note, and daycare or babysitting fees. These figures usually remain the same throughout the year unless there is an increase in your rent or changes to your taxes that will affect your mortgage payment. Some fixed expenses can be quarterly depending on how you choose to make your payments. For example, my disability and life insurance premiums are quarterly. List all of the expenses regardless of whether you pay monthly or quarterly. Later on, we will discuss how to account for these non-monthly expenses. Next, you will want to list your variable expenses. This is where it gets a bit difficult because variable expenses are not necessarily the same each month, and they could take up a good portion of your monthly spending. A good example would be grocery expenses. You may budget about $500 per month, but it may vary depending on extenuating circumstances. So, one month it may be $500, but it may be $700 the following month because you had visitors and you provided meals. Retrieve your previous statements and totals of your groceries and dining out expenses for a full twelve months and then divide by twelve. That should give you an idea of how much you should attribute to your monthly grocery and dining out expenses per month.

2nd Step – Kim will need to review her financial reports and scores. Financial reports or statements that can assist with that are the following: a net worth statement, a monthly budget (actual versus revised), and recent credit reports. A credit report is critical for a number of reasons—1. To review what her creditors are reporting each month, 2. Serve as a summary of all her credit products including outstanding balances and payment history, and 3. Reveal her credit score, which she does not know.

Net Worth Statement – A net worth statement is a financial document that lists your assets or items that you own such as a home, cash or investment accounts, and your liabilities which are items that you owe such as a mortgage, car note, or credit cards. The difference equates to your net worth. Ideally, your net worth is positive; however, there are some cases where it may be negative, such as with a medical student who has student loans but no assets. This is Kim's net worth statement:

KIM'S NET WORTH STATEMENT			
Assets		**Liabilities**	
Home Value (Condo)	$ 300,000	Mortgage	$ 220,000
Cash	$ 3,000	Student Loans	$ 75,000
Car	$ 10,000	Car Loan	$ -
401K	$ 75,000	Credit Cards	$ 75,000
Other personal Property	$ 10,000		
		Total	
Total Assets	$ 398,000	**Liabilities**	$ 370,000
		Net Worth	$ 28,000
			(Total Assets - Total Liabilities)

Monthly Budget – a statement, usually monthly, that lists your income versus your expected expenses. The goal is to have your revenues equal expenses. More importantly, you should include allocations for savings and investing in your budget. A budget acts as a blueprint on how to allocate each dollar you earn.

KIM'S MONTHLY HOUSEHOLD AND PERSONAL BUDGET

Gross Income

__* Annual Salary $90,000__   __$ 7,500__

Expenses:

Taxes and 401K/403B

Federal Withholding	(1,147)
Social Security	(465)
Medicare	(108)
New York State Tax Withholding	(397)
SDI	(3)
401K/403B savings	(225)
Savings/Emergency Fund	-
Mortgage	(1,200)
Groceries/Dining out	(300)
Utilities (Cable, electric, gas)	(200)
Wireless telephone	(100)

Transportation		
Car Note	-	
Fuel	(160)	
Car Insurance	(100)	
Maintenance	(50)	
Credit Cards	(1,875)	
Student Loan	(300)	
Clothing (including purchases and dry cleaning)	(400)	
Personal Hygiene	(100)	
Entertainment	(200)	
Travel	(170)	
Expenses Subtotal	(7,500)	
		$ (7,500)
		$ -

ANALYSIS

After our analysis, it was apparent that Kim's budget was allocating a lot toward credit card payments, many of which were just the minimum payments. This is a sign of poor financial management for a number of reasons:

1. Large amount of balances.

2. Minimum-only payments. Kim admits to paying just minimum payments. When you pay just the minimum, you may end paying for one item for a period of twenty years or more. Minimum payments are comprised of a percentage of your total balance, not a fixed payment like a car note or personal loan, so you may be paying a credit balance indefinitely if you continue to make purchases on the card.

3. Exceedingly high utilization. In her case, Kim is using around 70 percent of her total available credit which means she is relying on credit to live or maintain her current lifestyle.

TIPS FOR MAINTAINING HEALTHY CREDIT SCORE AND CREDIT MANAGEMENT

Here are some tips I suggested:

1. Get a good understanding of what credit is, why you use it, and how to utilize it properly. A credit card is a financial instrument, usually an actual card issued by a bank, retail establishment, or financial establishment, allowing you to purchase goods or services on credit. Credit card usage is one of the most common causes of financial mismanagement and a leading reason many live beyond their means. Many people will purchase items using plastic for either convenience or because they do not have the cash on hand to buy it outright. Do not fall into this trap. Credit card usage can be utilized responsibly.

2. Check your credit reports frequently. It is important to check for errors. A credit report details your credit history. It lists everywhere you have lived and worked, all the credit card payments or loans you owe, payment information, and how many times you have applied for credit, liens, bankruptcy, and judgments. It really gives

you a snapshot of where you are in terms of your overall credit life. Creditors look at these credit reports to make decisions based on your credit worthiness. It is imperative to monitor your credit report regularly. It is not only for you to see where you stand, but it will also tell you if there is fraud or if someone opened up an account in your name. There are so many options for obtaining a credit report. There are various ways you can check your credit report. And due to the Federal Fair Credit Reporting Act (FCRA), "each of the nationwide credit reporting companies—Equifax, Experian, and TransUnion—is required to provide you with a free copy of your credit report, at your request, once every 12 months." Here is the contact information for each reporting company (9):

Experian: 1-888-397-3742, www.experian.com
P.O. Box 9595
Allen, TX 75013

TransUnion: 1-800-916-8800,
www.transunion.com
P.O. Box 1000
Chester, PA 19022

Equifax: 1-800-685-1111, www.equifax.com
P.O. Box 740256
Atlanta, GA 30374

Alternatively, everyone is entitled to receive one free credit report on an annual basis. You can order your report via annualcreditreport.com, or call 1-877-322-8228.

You are also entitled to a free report if a company takes adverse action against you, such as denying your application for credit, insurance, or employment based on information in your report. You must ask for your report within sixty days of receiving notice of the action. The notice will give you the name, address, and phone number of the credit reporting company. According the Federal Trade Commission (FTC), you are also "entitled to one free report a year if you're unemployed and plan to look for a job within 60 days, if you're on welfare, or if your report is inaccurate because of fraud, including identity theft" (10).

3. If you find an error on your credit report, what are the necessary steps to dispute them?

Create and mail a letter to dispute a credit report or submit an online dispute letter via the credit reporting agencies. The FTC.gov website provides a sample dispute template for your use.

Make sure to send your letter by certified mail, "return receipt requested," so you can document what the credit reporting company received. Remember to include copies of the applicable enclosures and save copies for your files. This may include receipts that prove a debt was paid or that list the actual price paid for an item.

Also, keep copies of the letters you send to the credit reporting agencies for your records.

Once the credit reporting agency receives your dispute, they must adhere to the following:

They have thirty days to investigate any items that you have disputed; they must ask whoever provided the disputed item to investigate your claim and report back to the credit reporting agency. If the item is found to be a mistake, correction must be made by the entity who submitted the incorrect information. The credit reporting agency must provide the results in writing and provide you a free copy of your corrected credit report. Per the Illinois Legal Aid Online organization, the credit reporting agency must send you the name, address, and telephone number of the information provider for the item you are disputing; and at your request, the credit reporting agency is required to send correction notices to anyone who received your credit report in the past six months (two years if the report was for employment purposes). According to the organization, if you still do not feel that your dispute is resolved after the investigation, you can ask the credit reporting agencies to include a statement of your dispute in your file and future credit reports. You can also ask them to give your statement of dispute to any organizations that were given your credit report in the recent past. There may be a fee for that, however.

4. Set up auto pay for your credit card bills and always pay more than the minimum. This will reduce balances faster.

5. Keep credit card balances low. Keep utilization below 30 percent. This means: keep your outstanding balance at 30 percent of your total credit line. For example, it your total credit limits are $100,000, your outstanding balances should be no more than $30,000. Better yet, paying your

balances in full each month which will keep interest payments nonexistent.

Monitor your FICO/Vanguard score. A FICO/Vanguard score is like a report card of your credit worthiness. A good credit score is GOLD! Every aspect of your financial life is affected by your FICO score. With a good credit score (anything over 670), you will normally get great interest rates on car notes or mortgages and have an easier time renting an apartment and establishing utilities in your name without a down payment or receiving better insurance rates. Your credit score is comprised of the following:

a) **Payment history.** Your payment history comprises 35 percent of your total score and is considered to be an important component of the score. Before credit can be extended, potential creditors want to have assurance that you pay your credit bills on time.

b) **Balances due.** The amount that you owe comprises about 30 percent of your total score. Creditors review not only the total amount but also the total amount in relation to your total credit limits. If you are maxed out, meaning you are utilizing all of your credit lines to the maximum limit, your creditors may conclude you are overextended and relying too heavily on borrowed money which increases your risk factor to default on your obligation.

c) **Credit history length.** This accounts for 15 percent of your credit score. The longer you have held credit the better. It is usually an indication that you have experience with credit. A person with no credit or recent credit (such as establishing credit of only four months) is considered riskier than someone who has established credit for over seven years.

d) **Credit mix.** Credit mix accounts for 10 percent of your credit score. Creditors like to see different types of credit on a profile such as credit cards, installment accounts, retail credits, and automobile and mortgage loans.

e) **New credit.** New credit accounts for 10 percent of your credit score. Opening a slew of new accounts especially in a short period of time is a red flag according to creditors.

f) **By the way, what is a good credit score?**

A credit score ranges from 350 to 850. Here is a break down:

A credit score range under 350 – chances are this borrower has no credit and would need to establish a credit history. Obtaining a secured credit card with a small credit limit ($300 to $500) would be a great start.

A range from 350 to 579 is considered "poor" – a score in this range would make obtaining credit difficult because the creditor may consider the borrower to be risky. A person with a score in this range should work diligently to improve this score, perhaps working with a financial counselor.

A range from 580 to 669 is considered "fair" – with a score in this range, borrowers may have the ability to obtain credit but most likely will incur higher rates and associated fees.

A range from 670 to 739 is considered "good" – Most American consumers have a credit score within this range. Most credit products such as consumer loans or credit cards will carry competitive interest rates.

A range from 740 to 799 is considered "very good" – a consumer with a score in this range usually will obtain credit products at very good interest rates. These borrowers are considered to be very responsible with credit and have a good payment history, good credit mix, low credit or loan balances in relation to total credit limits and lengthy credit history length.

A range from 800 to 850 is considered "excellent" – borrowers with credit scores in this range are considered to be exceptional credit consumers with an extremely low credit default risk. These consumers usually receive optimal interest rates on credit products such as credit cards, personal and car loans, and mortgages.

6. Do not close credit card accounts, especially older accounts. Your credit score is dependent on the age of credit card accounts. Accounts opened for over ten years contribute positively to your credit score.

PLAN

After reviewing her budget and outstanding credit card balance, Kim made a commitment to pay off the total credit card balance of $75,000 over a three-year period. She will be able to accomplish this by reducing several line items in her budget. Her priority is retirement savings, and she knows she must become serious about paring down spending. She pays nearly $1,875 a month in minimum payments. It will take her nearly forever to pay off balances since minimum payments are calculated on a percentage of her balance. Her revised budget is below.

KIM'S REVISED MONTHLY HOUSEHOLD AND PERSONAL BUDGET

Gross Income

* Annual Salary $90,000   **$ 7,500**

Expenses:

Taxes and 401K/403B

Federal Withholding	(1,147)
Social Security	(465)
Medicare	(108)
New York State Tax Withholding	(397)
SDI	(75)
401K/403B savings	
Savings/Emergency Fund	-
Mortgage	(1,200)
Groceries/Dining out	(300)
Utilities (Cable, electric, gas)	(200)
Wireless telephone	(100)
Transportation	
Car Note	-
Fuel	(160)
Car Insurance	(100)
Maintenance	(50)

Credit Cards	(2,600)	
Student Loan	(300)	
Clothing (including purchases and dry cleaning)	(150)	
Personal Hygiene	(100)	
Entertainment	(50)	
Travel	-	
Expenses Subtotal	(7,502)	
		$ (7,502)
		$ (2)

Kim decided to reduce her clothing, entertainment, and travel budget line items and put retirement savings on temporary hold. She figured she would get more return on her money if she paused retirement savings and eliminate her credit card debt with the high interest rates.

Old budget line items:

401K/403B savings	(225)
Credit Cards	(1,875)
Student Loan	(300)
Clothing (including purchases and dry cleaning)	(400)
Personal Hygiene	(100)
Entertainment	(200)
Travel	(170)

New budget line items:

401K/403B savings	
Credit Cards	(2,600)
Student Loan	(300)
Clothing (including purchases and dry cleaning)	(150)
Personal Hygiene	(100)
Entertainment	(50)
Travel	-

Kim has concluded that her goals are achievable based on where she stands and what she is able to allocate toward her debt reduction goal. We will continue to meet, and I will continue to be an accountable partner to her.

NOTES

NOTES

NOTES

CHAPTER 3

Family Saving for College

Education is the passport to the future, for tomorrow belongs to those who prepare for it today.

—Malcolm X

NEW BABY – HOW DO WE SAVE FOR COLLEGE?

New parents Veronica and George come to my office for financial counseling. The couple is in their thirties and have been married for two years. Veronica is now eight months pregnant, and the parents are discussing future plans regarding their child's education. Veronica is a sales manager at a department store, and George is an IT professional for their local college. They have a combined income of $150,000 and own a home. Debt profile is: mortgage, car loans, and a small amount of student debt and savings/investments. They have the same mindset regarding spending; both are savers and somewhat frugal. George is due for a promotion that will increase his yearly salary by 20 percent, which the family plans to allocate to college savings and retirement savings. They believe the timing of the promotion is perfect considering the new baby is on the way, which not only translates to newfound joy to the family but also expenses. They consider themselves fortunate to also have Veronica's mother available to babysit the infant when Veronica decides to return to work after a three month maternity leave. The couple has great insurance that will cover Veronica's pregnancy medical costs and the family's health care. According to the couple, the main concern is savings.

THE ISSUES

Not many! After we gathered their information, I concluded that they were in great shape. They were adequately saving 10 percent of their income, had a nice emergency fund saved, and had little debt. In addition, they lived close to family who will help support the new family and baby.

DISCUSSION OF GOALS

The goals are to pay off their home in fifteen years (currently two years into a thirty-year mortgage) and pay off car loans within one year. Since their main concern is college savings, we discussed various options.

STEPS

Education! We discussed the various options available to them including the 529 plan.

WHAT IS A 529 PLAN?

According to the U.S. Securities and Exchange Commission (SEC)'s Office of Investor Education and Advocacy Investor Bulletin: "A 529 plan is a tax-advantaged savings plan designed to encourage saving for future education costs. 529 plans, legally known as 'qualified tuition plans,' are sponsored by states, state agencies, or educational institutions and are authorized by Section 529 of the Internal Revenue Code" (4).

There are two types of 529 plans: prepaid tuition plans and education savings plans. Here are the explanations for both that illustrate the similarities and the differences.

PREPAID 529 TUITION PLAN

The purchaser of the plan obtains credits from a college or university in today's dollars that will be applied to future tuition and fees on behalf of a beneficiary. However, these credits cannot be applied to room and board. These credits also cannot be applied toward elementary or secondary school tuition. These plans can usually charge administration fees.

Another aspect is the credits are not guaranteed by the federal government, and some states may guarantee these credits, but there are some who do not. So, what does this mean? This means that if the university or college is unable to fulfill this end of the contract for whatever reason including financial insolvency, the purchaser may lose their credits or money.

Plans may have enrollment and age limitations. For example, there may be a state residency requirement or you also may only enroll in the savings plan at certain times of the year.

529 EDUCATION SAVINGS PLAN

The purchaser opens an investment account such as a mutual fund or other financial bank product. Some of these monies may be protected by the Federal Deposit Insurance Corporation (FDIC), but monies invested in mutual funds accounts are not protected. So, this consideration should be accounted for when you open these accounts. You can use a broker or open an account on your own at one of the financial institutions that offers these savings plan. The interest on these funds grows tax-free, meaning you do not pay taxes on the accumulated balance. Unlike the prepaid tuition plans, these monies not only can be used toward tuition fees, but they can also be applied toward room and board.

Another difference from the prepaid plans is that these monies, up to $10,000, can be used toward elementary and secondary schools such as middle or high schools.

State governments sponsor these educational savings plans but do not guarantee them. However, there are no age or enrollment requirements. And seldom are there residency requirements, meaning a Kentucky parent or grandparent can establish a New York state 529 plan.

PLAN

Veronica and George seemed overly excited about the 529 plans for college savings; however, they wanted to learn about other options. So, we discussed other options, but they were definitely leaning toward the 529 plans.

SCHOLARSHIPS

So, what are the other options for college savings? Of course, another option is scholarships. If your child is academically or athletically talented, there are scholarships that may be applicable to them. There are many sources for scholarship funds—for example, your employers or religious or social organizations like sororities or fraternities. Scholarships may be recommended by high school officials such as guidance counselor or teachers. The college a student is accepted to may have scholarships available to students. When I was a medical student, some of my classmates were recipients of scholarships that covered not all but a large majority of medical school expenses such as tuition and fees.

An internet search can yield a trove of information. Here is a list of websites that provide scholarship information:

- www.studentsavingsguide.com

- www.earntolearn.org

- www.savingforcollege.com/

- www.militaryonesource.mil
  (for children of those serving in the military)

- https://myscholly.com/

LOCAL COLLEGES INCLUDING COMMUNITY COLLEGE

As of the writing of this book, many states have tuition-free college. There are eleven, with many other states considering enacting the same. The current states include New York, New Jersey, Maryland, Delaware, Oregon, Rhode Island, Nevada, Kentucky, Arkansas, Indiana, and Tennessee. In any case, attending an in-state college/university or community college can cost significantly less than attending an out-of-state school. A strategy I discuss often is considering a community college for the first half of college and transferring to a four-year college to complete a bachelor's degree. Significant savings can be realized with this approach if finances are an issue.

FINANCIAL AID

Depending on your family's economic status, a child may be able to obtain financial aid. Financial aid is a package comprised of loans, grants, college work study, and even scholarships. In order to apply for financial aid, you must fill out a FAFSA which stands for Free Application for Federal Student Aid. This application allows you to apply for the options above all on one form, and once accepted, the school will determine your federal aid eligibility which is based on a variety of factors such as cost of attendance (this includes tuition, room and board, books and fees) and expected family contribution. Once you graduate, the federal loans—whether they are subsidized or unsubsidized—must be paid back usually starting six months after you graduate.

PRIVATE LOANS

If there is still a gap or you do not qualify for federal financial aid, you may be able to take out private loans. These loans are usually based on credit worthiness.

PARENTAL LOANS

Parents may have an option to obtain a loan on behalf of their child. These loans are called PLUS loans and are federal loans. The lender is the federal government and loan eligibility is based on your credit profile and other requirements.

CONCLUSION

Veronica and George walked away from the session fully aware of their options and plan to start a 529 fund as soon as their baby is born.

Cheers to a great and prosperous future Veronica, George, and new baby!

NOTES

NOTES

NOTES

CHAPTER 4

Student Loans

*When the time came for me to go to college,
there was only one scholarship that my high school
offered at the time and I didn't win that one, but
that didn't stop me. I went on to college anyway.
I worked my way through it and paid my student
loans for 11 years.*

—Chandra Wilson

Ughhh, school loans are the bane of many people's existence. Actually, these loans amount to the tune of 1.6 trillion dollars according to the Federal Reserve Board. However, when I think of my student loans, I attempt to think of them as an investment. If it weren't for my loans, I would not have been able to become a physician because it was student loans that financed my medical school education. I love what I do, so I do not think of them as a burden especially since I make enough money to pay them down and soon off! So, I have a different mindset. However, that does not mean I want to remain married to them forever. I desire to pay them off because it will free up a substantial part of my income to apply to other financial goals I have for myself, such as retirement, real estate, and charity among other things.

Meet Beth. She shares my sentiments, but she is younger and would like to eliminate her student loans sooner rather than later because she desires to have a home and would like to invest in real estate in the not-so-distant future. Beth just graduated from graduate school and has about $150,000 in federal subsidized and unsubsidized student loans and plans to eliminate her debt in less than ten years. She is currently twenty-four years of age, and this is her only debt. Her loans for simplicity's sake are at 3 percent interest rate which is a great rate. She is a lawyer and accepted a position with an annual salary of $125,000. She plans to devote a significant chunk to her loans. She still lives at home with her parents and will just be responsible for a cable bill and some other small household expenses, since her parents' home is paid off. We reviewed various options, strategies, and the different student loan repayment options.

Let's look at the various repayment options:

Standard Repayment Plan – This is the standard ten-year repayment plan. With this payment plan, she will pay fixed payments or 120 payments of the same amount. Since it is paid off within a relatively short period of time, she will most likely save money on interest. She currently does not qualify for Public Service Loan Forgiveness because she is working for a private law firm, so this may be a great option since her priority is to pay off the $150,000. Her approximate payment under this plan would be $1,500 per month.

Graduated Repayment Plan – Under this plan, the borrower pays a minimal amount (less than the standard repayment amount), and the payments gradually increase. Usually, these loans can be paid off within ten years.

Extended Repayment Plan – Under this plan, the borrower, who has to have more than $30,000 in loans, makes payments that ensure satisfaction of loan within twenty-five years. Her loans under this amount would be approximately $700 per month.

Revised Pay As You Earn Repayment Plan (RE-PAYE) – Under this plan, the borrower's monthly payments are based on 10 percent of discretionary income. Each year the borrower must recertify to the payment plan based on current income and family size, and if the borrower is married, combined income will be considered. After twenty or twenty-five years (if these are graduate loans), the loan may be forgiven, and the amount forgiven may be taxable.

Income Based Repayment Plan (IBR) – Under this plan, the borrower's monthly payments are based on 10 to 15 percent of discretionary income since there is a high debt-to-income ratio. Each year the borrower must recertify the payment plan based on current income and family size, and if the borrower is married, combined income will be considered. After twenty or twenty-five years (depending on when you established the loans), the loan may be forgiven, and the amount forgiven may be taxable.

Income Contingent Repayment Plan (ICR) – This loan is available for Direct Loans. Under this plan, the borrower's monthly payment is based on either 20 percent of discretionary income or fixed payments based on a twelve-year time frame, whichever results in the lesser monthly payment amount. Each year, the borrower must recertify the payment plan based on current income and family size, and if the borrower is married, combined income will be considered. After twenty-five years the loan may be forgiven, and the amount forgiven may be taxable.

Income Sensitive Repayment Plan – This payment plan is only available for Federal Family Education Loan (FFEL) borrowers. Under this plan, the borrower pays a monthly payment based on income, but the loan has a repayment term of fifteen years.

OTHER OPTIONS

Some other options borrowers who qualify can explore:

LOAN FORGIVENESS

Some examples are the PSLF or the Public Service Loan Forgiveness plan, which is a loan forgiveness plan that allows a borrower to have outstanding loans forgiven if 120 payments are made while working full-time for a qualifying employer, usually a nonprofit or government agency. These loans must be Direct Loans, and the borrower would need to make payments under a qualifying repayment plan such as Income Based Repayment Plan (IBR) or Revised Pay As You Earn Repayment Plan (REPAYE).

LOAN REPAYMENT

Health care primary care professionals may be eligible for loan repayment under the National Health Service Corps. Employers may offer loan repayment incentives for employment. Look for state repayment programs.

MILITARY SERVICE

At one point, I considered enlisting in the military to satisfy my loans. This may be an option if serving your country appeals to you.

COMMON REPAYMENT STRATEGIES

- Apply financial windfalls such as an income tax refund or bonus to student loans.

- If married and each spouse works, live off of one income and utilize the other to pay down student loans.

- Move to a low-cost area of the country. If you live in a high-cost area of the country like New York City or San Francisco, move to an area where the cost of living is less. The money saved, especially if income remains the same, can be used to reduce student loan debt.

- Find a side hustle or start a business and utilize the extra income toward loan repayment.

- Move back home and apply savings to loan repayment.

- Reduce living expenses such as cable, other entertainment, and dining expenses.

- Refinance your student loans if loans are at a high interest rate. SoFi offers refinancing for qualified borrowers, especially those with good credit and low debt-to-income ratio.

With these options, Beth walked away feeling confident that she will be student loan debt-free well within her ten-year time frame.

NOTES

_____

_____

_____

_____

_____

_____

_____

_____

_____

_____

_____

_____

_____

_____

_____

_____

_____

_____

NOTES

NOTES

CHAPTER 5

Insurance

*I don't call it "Life Insurance," I call it
"Love Insurance." We buy it because we want
to leave a legacy for those we love.*

—**Farshad Asl**

Throughout our lifetimes, we work, save a portion of our incomes, purchase assets, and make a living for our loved ones. Unless individuals are financially independent, most of us rely on insurance to provide protection to our assets such as car, personal property, home, and income. In many cases, we look for this protection so that we can provide money to those we care about such as a spouse or significant other, children, or favorite charity. These people or entities are called beneficiaries.

Let us meet Pamala. Pamala is feeling a bit over-whelmed as of late. Pamala is a forty-year-old married woman with three children. Pamala is a CEO executive assistant who makes a salary of $80,000, and her husband makes $100,000 as a nurse. Pamala has a seventy-year-old mother, Brenda, who is recently widowed. Pamala's father recently died of a stroke at the age of sixty-nine. Unfortunately, Pam's father did not have insurance so Pamala and her siblings had to foot the bill for the funeral services. Her mother continues to work part-time at a department store, bringing in about $24,000 per year. Luckily, Brenda's home is paid in full; she is responsible for property taxes of $6,000 per year. Her taxes are so low due to her state's senior citizens tax abatement, which shaves $3,000 from her yearly taxes. Brenda has no debt and has accumulated about $150,000 in retirement funds which are in conservative mutual funds of mostly treasury and municipal securities due to the tax advantage. Pamala and her husband are considering asking Brenda to move in with her to assist in offsetting costs and possibly sell her home, with profits added to her mother's retirement funds. However, Brenda enjoys her independence and feels she is comfortable financially. She receives about $1,600 per month in social security in addition to her part-time salary. She enjoys traveling and entertaining friends and family. The family lives in a low cost of living area of Georgia.

Pamala is thinking long-term. She knows her mother is fairly healthy and could sustain her currently lifestyle with her social security and part-time salary. But her father's death was a jolt to her system and made her think about the future in terms of her financial viability and her mother's as well. With the cost of long-term care, which can range from $20,000 to more than $90,000 annually, her mother's current retirement savings could last from seven to less than three years depending on the services needed. Her father also didn't leave a will nor had he had life insurance because he was the type of person who never wanted to discuss those matters.

Pamala and her husband, Mike, decided to have a heart-to-heart with Brenda to discuss future plans and decided to take a hard look at their situation going forward.

AFTER THE FAMILY MEETING

Pamala and Mike realized they had life insurance and disability insurance through their employers but no stand-alone policies. They have three young children ages fifteen, nine, and seven. They have six months of emergency funds to cover expenses should there be a disruption in either one's salary and about $200,000 combined in their 401k. They have a $300,000 mortgage balance, car notes of $600 per month combined for two cars, and about $10,000 in credit card balances. The kids are in private school, which equates to about $3,000 a month for all three children. Pamala and Mike also did not have a will nor a trust. They felt it was time to get these items in order, so they made appointments with a financial planner/insurance broker and attorney to get their insurance and estate affairs in order. They soon realized that choosing an insurance product was not going to be a cut-and-dried procedure. There are so many products. Let us review three main types of insurance policies:

FORMS OF LIFE INSURANCE

TERM LIFE INSURANCE

What it is: Insurance protection that is for a specified period of time. At the time of death, the beneficiary receives the face value of the policy. For example, for a thirty-year term life policy in the amount of $100,000, the specified time period is thirty years, and the face value is

100,000. If the holder of the policy dies within the thirty years, the beneficiary will receive the full $100,000. The policy remains in effect as long as premiums are paid during the term of the policy.

Main provisions: Depending on the policy, the premium may stay the same or increase, and face value may be level or decrease in value. There is no cash value component.

What makes it attractive: Term life insurance can be very inexpensive especially at a young age and in comparison to whole life insurance. However, a common provision is that it can convert to a whole life without a physical exam.

PERMANENT LIFE INSURANCE

WHOLE LIFE INSURANCE

What it is: A permanent life insurance that provides lifetime protection as long as premiums are paid as agreed.

Main provisions: It may have a cash value which increases to face value; however, it is different than the policy's face value which is the amount that is paid to your beneficiary. Once cash value increases to face value, the policy is paid in full, and no premium payments are due. An insured person may be able to take a loan against the cash value. However, the loan must be paid back with interest, or the death benefit to the beneficiary will be reduced. If the policy is surrendered, you may be able to receive the cash value. It is usually incorporated into estate planning.

Types:

❯ **Ordinary Life:** Premiums are paid until death or age 100.

❯ **Variable Life:** Cash values can be invested in stocks, bonds, or money market funds.

Advantages:

❯ Offers lifetime protection

❯ Cash value is tax-deferred

Disadvantages:

❯ Expensive in comparison to term life.

UNIVERSAL LIFE INSURANCE

What it is: A permanent life insurance policy that has an investment component/cash value and low premiums similar to a term policy.

DISCUSSION

How much insurance do Pamala and Mike need? The industry rule of thumb is twelve to sixteen times the amount of one's gross earnings. We also cannot forget about *disability insurance*. Unless you are independently wealthy, **everyone** should have disability insurance. Disability insurance replaces income if you are unable to work. There are two types—short-term and long-term. Short-term covers usually about 60 to 70 percent of your current income and will cover for a period less than six months. Long-term will cover up to 60 to 70 percent of your current income depending on the policy but may be as low as 40 percent. The younger you are the less your premium is, and the premium is also dependent on your monthly payout. The payment may be taxed depending on terms of the policy, who paid the premiums, and how payments were made. If your employer paid the premiums, the monthly benefit may be taxable. If you paid the premiums with after tax dollars, then generally the monthly benefit is not taxable.

Although the couple plans to meet with an estate attorney for estate planning, they want to get a foundation for preparation for their upcoming meeting.

What exactly is estate planning? Estate planning is basically the planning in advance of your wishes and disposition of your assets in the event of your incapacitation or death. Of course, it is much more than that; it should include the following:

- Provisions for your minor children, especially children with special needs. Includes the naming of a guardian in the event you are the sole custodian of your children.

- Instruction for your health care in the event you are unable to make decisions because you are either disable or incapacitated.

- Provisions on how your business will be handled in the event of your incapacitation or death.

- Provision of ways to minimize taxes and other costs such as legal costs.

Everyone can have an estate plan—it is not just for the wealthy; it is for anyone with any kind of asset, which would be everyone. That includes furniture, cars, clothing, jewelry, artwork, books, a business, or anything that has value to the holder. Without planning, the assets of the deceased end up in limbo, with the state deciding how the assets should be distributed. This is called dying "intestate." Therefore, it is important to make your wishes known and official. There are many different ways to accomplish that. It begins with either a will or a trust. There are certain events that necessitate a need for an estate plan:

- ❯ Getting married

- ❯ Having a child

- ❯ Getting a divorce

- ❯ Starting a business

- ❯ Death of a spouse

- ❯ Getting an inheritance or some other lump sum of money

- ❯ Onset of a disability

There are a couple of main components to estate planning. An estate plan will be inclusive of the following:

- ❯ A *will* or *trust*. A *will* is a legal document that specifies how you want your affairs handled and how you want your possessions distributed in the event of your death. A will is a critical part of estate planning and should be established with the help of an estate attorney. A *trust* is a fiduciary relationship where a trustee is given permission by you to handle your assets such as a home or investments on behalf of your designated beneficiaries. There are many types of trusts, but for the purposes of this discussion, we will discuss a living trust, which is a trust that is created while the trustor is alive. Like a will, a trust states how you want your assets transferred and other wishes, but the main difference between a will and living trust is that once a person dies, both the will and the trust comes into effect, but a will has to go through *probate* which is a legal or court process that verifies and ensures that your wishes are carried out and that assets are distributed to your heirs and beneficiaries as you specified. Probate can be expensive due to court fees, and it may take some time, as long as six to nine months. If a person dies without a will, the probate court decides how the property should be distributed. A person can bypass probate by placing their property in a living trust. Do you need both a living trust and a will? Yes, because you most likely will not transfer or cannot transfer all of your property to a trust, for example, items you may receive right before death. Or if you want to name a guardian to care for your children in the event of your death, you must specify that wish in a will; you cannot do that in a trust.

- A **power of attorney**—a document which names someone to make decisions on behalf of another person. There are different types of POAs; you can have a medical POA (in this case the person named in the document would make decisions on your health care in the event you are incapacitated) or a financial POA (in this case the person named in document would make decisions on your finances in the event you are incapacitated).

- An **advance health care directive.** An advance health care directive is a legal document that goes into effect only if you are incapacitated and unable to speak for yourself. It is comprised of a healthcare POA; sometimes the person is referred to as the health care proxy. This is the person that makes medical decisions when you are unable to. A **living will** is a legal document that specifies your medical care wishes when you are unable to communicate your wishes.

- Selecting your fiduciaries who are persons or organizations that act on behalf of another person or persons is important. They are required to place the interest of their clients ahead of their own, with a duty to preserve good faith and trust. They are required to act both legally and ethically in the other person's interest. You can have a trust fiduciary or an investment fiduciary as in an investment advisor or an executor of a will or a lawyer.

- Selecting your beneficiaries. Your beneficiary is the person(s) who will receive your assets named in a trust, will, or even an insurance policy.

Pam and Mike walked away with enough information to start the process of making a thorough and educated decision regarding asset protection and estate planning.

NOTES

NOTES

NOTES

NOTES

CHAPTER 6

Investing

Wealth is the ability to fully experience life.

—Henry David Thoreau

Sandy, a mother, age sixty, and her daughter Sandra, age thirty, decided they wanted to meet with me to discuss their investment options. They are in great financial shape. Both are employed, and they contribute the maximum amount to their 401k; however, the mother contributes an additional $6,000 because she is over the age of fifty. Due to the sound financial foundation provided to her by her mother, Sandra understands the importance of not accumulating a great deal of debt. She has student loan debt of $50,000 and no credit card debt. Two years ago, she obtained employment with a company that has loan forgiveness of $10,000 per year. She continues to make payments on her loan in addition to the

$10,000. Her plan is to complete her loan repayment in three years. Both Sandy and Sandra have no car loans—both loans were paid off after two and three years, respectively. They both have emergency funds with six months of expenses saved. Sandra lives in a condo with a loan payment of $1,500 per month and Sandy lives in a home that is paid off but pays quarterly property taxes of $6,000.

Now that they have the emergency fund and debt and expenses under control, they are ready to invest. They are interested in stocks, bonds, and real estate.

Before one can invest, Sandy and Sandra must evaluate the following: their goals and risk tolerance.

I prepared a risk tolerance questionnaire that evaluates a client's willingness to take on risks. It helps to determine whether Sandy and Sandra are risk-averse or risk-tolerant. This will determine what products the two will invest in.

Here are the questions they received:

- If a volatile stock market is down 30 percent, what percentage of your portfolio are you willing to lose?

- On a scale of 1 to 10, rank your understanding of the stock market.

- ❯ On a scale of 1 to 10, rank your comfort level with investing in the stock market.

- ❯ What sort of return do you want on your investment portfolio?

- ❯ At what point in time do you expect to utilize invested capital?

- ❯ How much do you have in an emergency fund, and how many months of expenses does it cover?

- ❯ What are your short-term, intermediate term, and long-term financial goals?

In addition to investing in individual stocks in a company, most people start investing in mutual funds by type. Here are several different types of investment products the mother/daughter duo can invest in:

Small-cap funds include investment in stocks in companies with a total stock value between $300 million and $2 billion. These companies are usually riskier than mid-cap and large-cap funds.

Mid-cap funds include investment in companies with stock value between $2 billion to $10 billion in market capitalization or total stock value.

Large-cap funds include investment in stocks in the largest companies in the world, with market capitalization over $10 billion. These companies include Apple, Microsoft, Amazon and Facebook.

Foreign equity funds, or global/international funds include investment in foreign stocks. These funds are more high-risk but may bring in higher returns.

Fixed income funds (also known as bond funds) are comprised of financial products of debt issued by local and national governments and large companies. Fixed income funds are considered low risk.

A balanced funds (also called hybrid funds) include both stocks or equity and bond financial products.

Index funds: An index fund is a fund such as a mutual fund or exchange-traded fund (ETF) that follows the performance of a particular market such as the S&P 500. These funds normally have low fees and expenses.

Yay! The duo has calculated their net worth and budget, set their goals including their savings goals, and eliminated debt. So, naturally, their next step will be focused on investing. Investing is where real growth of wealth comes from.

Why is saving and investing so important and critical to financial success and independence?

The earlier you start saving and investing, the more you reap. Why? It is due to a concept called **compounding interest**. According to investors.gov, "compound interest is the interest you earn on interest. This can be illustrated by using basic math: if you have $100 and it earns 5% interest each year, you will have $105 at the end of the first year. At the end of the second year, you will have $110.25. Not only did you earn $5 on the initial $100 deposit, but you also earned $0.25 on the $5 in interest" (5). My friend Karen from *Ladynomics* decided to take the $200 allocation from her budget and deposit it into a mutual fund account with an average six percent interest rate of return on investment; in twenty years, that investment will be worth $88,000! That is a significant amount of money. And it is all due to steady, regular investments over a period of time.

One important aspect of investing is understanding your risk. Some investors are conservative, meaning they have a low tolerance for losses; some don't mind investing in more aggressive funds, meaning they have a higher risk tolerance, and some are like me, who is in the middle.

Here are some guidelines for your review. However, make sure to sit with a trusted financial advisor or accountant because individual financial situations differ from one person to another.

AGGRESSIVE INVESTOR

An aggressive investor would be more open to increased risk for higher returns. You would expect a portfolio heavy in stock and light in bonds. For example, a mutual fund type portfolio may look like this: 20 percent fixed income (bonds) and 80 percent stocks comprised of 25 percent large cap funds, 25 percent foreign mutual funds, 20 percent each mid-cap and small-cap mutual funds.

MODERATE INVESTOR

With a moderate investor, you would expect a portfolio heavy in stock but not as much as the aggressive investor. The mutual fund portfolio presents like this: 35 percent fixed income (bonds) and 60 percent stocks (comprised of 30 percent large-cap funds, 15 percent foreign mutual funds, and 15 percent each mid-cap/small-cap mutual funds) and 5 percent money market funds.

CONSERVATIVE INVESTOR

With a conservative investor, you would expect a portfolio heavy with bonds which are less risky than stocks. The mutual fund portfolio may present like this: 50 percent fixed income (bonds) and 25 percent stocks (with a mix of large-cap funds, foreign mutual funds, mid-cap/small-cap mutual funds) and 25 percent in cash or money market funds.

Sandy and Sandra feel confident about mutual funds. But what they are also interested in investing in is individual stocks. But how do they go about it?

One of the first steps when evaluating a stock is to find one you are interested in and do research! The internet holds tons of information available for one to make an informed decision. You can start by looking at the financial statements of a company. All publicly traded companies must release financial statements. The main statements are the balance sheet, income statement, statement of cash flows, and the financial notes.

Balance Sheet – A balance sheet is a statement that lists a company's assets, liabilities, and shareholder's equity at a particular point in time. The difference between the total assets and liabilities equals the shareholder's equity. The assets are what a company owns such as cash, investments, account receivables, property, and even intangible items such as goodwill. The liabilities are what a company owes. These items include wages payable, accounts payable, interest payable, and bank loans. The balance sheet is especially important because the statement can tell someone how much debt a company owes. This information should be compared to previous reporting periods, and it should also be compared to the balance sheet of a company's competitors. Important financial ratios are derived from information from the balance sheet. A balance sheet is analogous to the net worth statement of an individual.

Income Statement – An income statement is also known as profit and loss statement (P&L) or statement of revenue and expenses. Revenues are either from operating revenue or income derived from the services or products sold from a business's activities; non-operating revenue is income derived from non-core business activities such as income earned from investments or rent from real estate or property for example. Expenses are associated with the costs associated with the main business activities such as cost of goods associated with services or products sold, wage expenses, and utilities. Expenses can also include interest paid on a loan. The difference between revenue and expenses is net income. Just as with the balance sheet, important financial ratios can be derived from information from the income statement.

Statement of Cash Flows – This is a statement that includes all the cash that the company made via operating activities from the business, financing derived from the issuance of equity or debt, and investing activities such as investment gains and losses. It shows how well a company manages cash and how well it manages its financial obligations. Cash at the end of year should equal end of year cash balance on the balance sheet.

For illustrative purposes only

	2020		2019		Variance**	
XYZ Company _(Comparative Balance Sheet, For the Years Ended December 31, 2020 and 2019)_						
Assets						
Cash	$	100,000	$	75,000	$	25,000
Accounts Receivable	$	300,000	$	375,000	$	(75,000)
Property	$	1,000,000	$	1,000,000	$	-
Inventory	$	250,000	$	125,000	$	125,000
Total Assets	$	1,550,000	$	1,500,000	$	50,000
Liabilities and Equity						
Accounts Payable	$	100,000	$	125,000	$	(25,000)
Wages Payable	$	300,000	$	275,000	$	25,000
Retained Earnings	$	1,250,000	$	1,225,000	$	25,000
Total Liabilities and Equity	$	1,550,000	$	1,500,000	$	25,000
** Explained in Notes						

ABC Company
Comparative Income Statement
For the Years Ended December 31, 2020 and 2019

		2020		2019		Variance**
Revenues:						
Sales	$	2,000,000	$	1,750,000	$	250,000
Total Revenues	$	2,000,000	$	1,750,000	$	250,000
Operating Expenses:						
Cost of Sales	$	(1,000,000)	$	(875,000)	$	(125,000)
Marketing	$	(400,000)	$	(325,000)	$	(75,000)
Wages and Other administrative costs	$	(200,000)	$	(180,000)	$	(20,000)
Total Operating Expenses	$	(1,600,000)	$	(1,380,000)	$	(220,000)
Other Income (Expense)						$ -
Interest Income	$	30,000	$	27,000	$	3,000
Interest Expense	$	(15,000)	$	(20,000)	$	5,000
Total Other Income (Expense)	$	15,000	$	7,000	$	8,000
Income before income taxes	$	415,000	$	377,000	$	38,000
Provision for income taxes	$	(83,000)	$	(75,400)	$	(7,600)
Net Income	$	332,000	$	301,600	$	30,400

** Explained in Notes

123 Company
Statement of Cash Flows
For the Year Ended December 31, 2020

		2020
Operating Activity		
Net Income	$	200,000
Increase in account receivable	$	75,000
Net Cash provided in operating activity	$	275,000
Investing Activity	$	10,000
Financing	$	20,000
Net Increase in Cash	$	305,000
Cash at beginning of year		0
Cash at the end of year	$	305,000

Financial Notes – Additional information regarding the operations of the business are explained in the notes section. Here you will find explanation for large year-by-year differences, of unusual changes in business activities or the industry as a whole, and it may contain supplemental reports. Critical information may be found in this section.

Company Prospectus – When a company is issuing stocks for the very first time, the company must file a report with the Securities Exchange Commission (SEC) called a prospectus. The prospectus provides a great deal of information about the security, financial statements, the executive, and other important information needed by potential investors.

Now that you have read and hopefully understand the financial statements, the next step would involve understanding performance ratios. These ratios can indicate the financial health of a company and should also be used to also compare ratios with other companies in the same industry.

A couple of ratios to understand:

DEBT-TO-EQUITY RATIO (TOTAL LIABILITIES / SHAREHOLDERS EQUITY)

This ratio tells an investor how much a company is using debt for its assets and to fund its business operations.

RETURN ON EQUITY (ROE) (NET INCOME / SHAREHOLDER'S EQUITY)

This ratio indicates how well a company uses its assets to derive profits. It is important to compare this ratio to other companies within an industry.

EARNINGS PER SHARE (EPS) – (NET INCOME – PREFERRED DIVIDENDS / AVERAGE OUTSTANDING COMMON SHARES)

It is what is sounds like, meaning it is the portion of a company's profit assigned to each outstanding share of common stock. It can tell a great deal about the financial stability and health of a company. Again, it should be compared to other companies within an industry, but the higher the EPS the better.

NET PROFIT MARGIN (NET PROFIT / NET SALES)

A high net profit margin tells an investor how good a company is at converting revenues into profit. It tells you how well a company is at controlling costs. This number should be compared to other companies in the same industry.

DEBT TO ASSET (TOTAL LIABILITIES / TOTAL ASSETS)

This ratio takes a look at the proportion of total liabilities to assets. Naturally an investor would want this number to be low or less than "1" because it means that there are enough assets to cover liabilities in the event the company liquidates.

Of course, there are many more ratios to compute, but these are some of the main ones. Once you understand the core financial statements and ratios, the next step would be to consult with some of the financial sites, books, or magazines that provide financial analysts research and recommendations. Many of these reports will provide additional guidance and explanations of the happenings of a company. Some sites to follow include: Yahoo finance, Google Finance, Bloomberg, Wall Street Journal, CNBC, Market watch, Morningstar, Seeking Alpha and Motley Fool.

Both Sandy and Sandra feel they have a firm foundation to make the necessary steps to dip into the financial markets.

NOTES

NOTES

NOTES

NOTES

CHAPTER 7

Real Estate–A First-Time Homebuyer

Ninety percent of all millionaires become so through owning real estate.

—Andrew Carnegie

Being a first-time homebuyer is extremely exciting! If you have been renting a long time, you may decide that owning a home is the next logical step. Owning real estate is a great way to build wealth because real estate generally increases in value over time. In my childhood neighborhood, we have homes that sold for $35,000 in the early 1970s that now sell for nearly $500,000! There are a great deal of benefits from owning a home, but there are some costs as well.

Some of the advantages include:

1. As mentioned above—wealth building due to increased equity. In my example about the homes in my childhood neighborhood, the increase in equity is substantial.

2. Tax advantage. You can write off mortgage expenses and property taxes against your income. In the first year of your homeownership, the same year you took out a mortgage, you may write off mortgage points.

3. Stability—mortgage payments remain stable (safe from some increases in property taxes and insurance costs).

Some of the disadvantages include:

1. Costs. Owning a home can be expensive. One should never purchase a home for more than they can afford. Some costs associated with owning a home include maintenance costs such as landscaping or normal repairs. When you rent, all you need to cover is your rent and possibly utilities. Maintenance costs are covered by the landlord.

2. Home depreciation. Sometimes homes depreciate; it occurs when there is an economic downturn like the financial crisis in 2007/2008. During that time, homes depreciated in areas with multiple foreclosures resulting in a 10 percent to 20 percent decrease in property values.

3. Decreased flexibility. It is difficult to unload a home, at least it is not as easy as it is to leave or move between apartments.

Michelle, age 35, is single and interested in buying a home. She has no idea where to start. She nor her family has ever owned a home; thus, she would be a first-time homebuyer. She is seeking advice. She currently rents but is paying $2,200 per month, and she thinks this money would be best applied to a property of her own. Her salary is $100,000.

The first thing we did was develop a checklist. There are a couple of things that should be in order before embarking on home ownership.

CHECKLIST

> Get a copy of Michelle's credit report from all three credit bureaus which are Experian,

TransUnion, and Equifax. I also recommended she access FICO.com to get her credit scores. I said scores because there are different scores for different items such as a FICO score for mortgages, credit cards, and automobiles, and she needs to see where she stands.

- Tabulate total amount of debt she currently owes. This is imperative because mortgage lenders use a ratio called debt-to-income ratio (DTI) that looks at potential mortgage costs and total debt in comparison to your income. Most lenders, especially for conventional loans, do not want the total debt to be 43 percent (or 36 percent of income for conventional mortgages) of total gross income and do not want to see 28 percent of your income going toward mortgage including principal, interest, and insurance payments. If the ratio is too high, this may mean you are overextended and have too much debt. If it is low, lenders feel confident that the homebuyer will be able to cover costs including the mortgage payment.

DTI= Total of Monthly Debt Payments/Gross Monthly Income.

Based on her income of $100,000 and gross monthly income of $8,333, her debt-to-income (DTI) ratio for a conventional mortgage parameter would be 28 percent/36 percent or $2,333/$3,000. In other words, Michelle would be able to qualify for a mortgage with insurance, principal, and interest up to $2,333 and total debt including mortgage of $3,000. This DTI is the most conservative and may be adjusted depending on the final loan program she qualifies for.

- If a potential homebuyer has significant consumer debt, develop a payment plan to reduce that debt. In Michelle's case she has $5,000 in credit card debt, no car, or personal loans. It would work in her best interest to pay that debt off.

- Check savings. Most banks, especially in times of economic upheaval, want the potential homeowner to have at least 20 percent for a down payment and money to cover closing costs. However, these requirements are not set in stone. I have seen lenders accept smaller down payments, especially if they are for non-conventional mortgages, such as a Federal Housing Administration (FHA) loan, which is a mortgage that is insured by the FHA, or USDA loans and Veterans (VA) loans. Most lenders will allow a gift from a parent toward a down payment. Also, Michelle may be able to take out a loan or withdrawal from her 401k. However, if she makes this withdrawal, she will have to pay additional taxes on the amount and possibly a 10 percent penalty because she is younger than 59 ½ years of age. There are also many first-time homebuyer programs that provide down payment and closing cost assistance.

❯ Michelle also has to refrain from applying for new credit including credit cards or any type of loans.

❯ Research! She must do her research regarding the location where she wants to live for the true cost of homeownership there (it is not only mortgage) and various interest rate quotes from various banks.

❯ Get a preapproval. A preapproval may assist in the home bidding process.

NEXT STEP – SEARCH FOR YOUR HOME!

Make sure to use your heart and your head when looking for your home. Remember, owning a home is expensive with many hidden costs. Keep that in mind when looking for one. The goal is to find a home that you love, that is within your budget, and has minimal issues. It is critical to view all homes with a detective's eye and ask questions—as many as you can. Once you have established your budget, refer to this list of questions that you should ask (including questions that you should ask of the real estate agent you choose, the lender, and the seller) before and during the viewing:

OF THE SELLER:

- ❯ How long has this home been on the market?

- ❯ What is the condition of the home?

- ❯ Are all the appliances and fixtures included in the sale and if so, how old are they?

- ❯ Is there special insurance coverage you need for the home such as flooding or hurricane policies?

- ❯ Why are you selling the home?

- ❯ What is included in the home sale?

- ❯ Any significant damages to home due to a natural disaster or fire?

- ❯ Have there been insurance claims against the home?

- ❯ What is the neighborhood like?

- ❯ What are the average monthly utility costs?

- ❯ Are there any Homeowners Association (HOA) fees?

- ❯ How is the neighborhood? What is the makeup of homeowners? Are the neighbors primarily families, single families, or are there a lot of kids in the neighborhood?

OF THE REAL ESTATE AGENT:

- ❯ How long do you think it will take to find a home?

- ❯ What are recent sales in the area?

- ❯ Are you familiar with the neighborhood?

OF THE LENDER:

- ❯ What credit score do I need?

- ❯ Which type of mortgage could I qualify for?

- Based on the pre-approval mortgage amount or my budget, how much will my down payment and monthly payments be?

- What is the interest rate?

- What is the closing process and closing costs?

Once you find a home that you love and that is within your budget, the next step is to hire an inspector to examine the home. This is imperative, and this step should not be skipped. Here are the questions to ask, although a good inspector report will cover all bases regarding the home.

- How old is the roof, what is the condition, how many more years should the roof last?

- Are there any signs of water or fire damage?

- Is the electrical system safe and current?

- Are there plumbing issues or leaks?

- Are there any code issues?

- Are the following items present in the home?

  » Lead paint

  » Radon

» Mold

» Infestations such as termites

After searching for three months, Michelle found a home that she loved and thought was perfect. It passed inspection with very minor issues. Michelle made an offer, and it was accepted! Next she will meet with her attorney to have the contract reviewed; the deposit is collected, which is placed in escrow. Then she meets with the lender. During the process, the lender will recheck her credit and ask for appropriate documents for the loan. These documents include loan application, paycheck stubs, bank statements, other statements such as retirement accounts or investment accounts and whatever the lender requires. The lender will also require an appraisal of the home to make sure that the mortgage is covered by adequate collateral. During this time, you will incur closing costs as part of the deal. Closing costs are fees and charges due at the closing of a real estate deal; these are in addition to the purchase price of the property. Sellers also incur closing costs which are typically fees due to the real estate agent, i.e., a commission.

Closing costs may include some or all of the following and will be detailed on the loan estimate and closing disclosure which is required to be given to the buyer:

- ❯ Application Fee – a fee paid for applying for mortgage.

- ❯ Attorney Fee – fee paid for attorney.

- ❯ Closing Fee – fee paid to company, attorney, or escrow company, i.e., the party responsible for closing or completing the real estate transaction.

- ❯ Credit Report Fee – fee for credit report retrieval.

- ❯ Escrow Deposit – a deposit collected at the closing of the mortgage which is comprised of prepayments (usually two months of property tax and mortgage insurance).

- ❯ FHA Mortgage Insurance Premium – insurance premium levied by the Federal Housing Administration (FHA). It is usually 1.75 percent of the loan amount. It may be rolled into the mortgage depending on terms of mortgage.

- ❯ Flood Determination and Monitoring Fee – fee paid to determine if home is in a flood zone.

- Homeowners' Association Transfer Fee

- Homeowner's Insurance – insurance premium paid in advance for coverage on your home.

- Lender's Title Insurance – a fee paid to title company that provides protection should an issue arise regarding the title on the home.

- Lead-Based Paint Inspection – fee paid for inspection to ensure that home is free from lead paint.

- Points – a one-time fee paid to lender that lender charges to reduce interest rate. A point is equivalent to 1 percent of the loan balance.

- Owner's Title Insurance – protection paid to protect the deed of a homeowner against claims made against the deed based on the actions of the previous homeowner.

- Origination Fee – an administration fee charged by the lender.

- Pest Inspection – a fee some state and local governments require for pest inspection of the home.

- Prepaid Daily Interest Charges – prepaid interest which is calculated from the date of loan closing to the date of your first mortgage payment.

- Private Mortgage Insurance (PMI) – insurance paid by purchaser to lender if down payment is less than 20 percent. The lender charges this fee because they believe the loan is riskier than someone who has the financial ability to pay at least a 20 percent down payment.

- Property Appraisal Fee – fee paid for appraisal of property. The lender utilizes this information to determine the fair market value of the home. If the fair market value is less than the proposed mortgage, then the mortgage can be denied if the buyer is unable to make up the difference. For example, if the fair market value of a home is $300,000 but the home asking price is $330,000 and the bank requires a 10 percent down payment, the buyer has to come up with a down payment of $60,000 if the seller is unwilling to reduce the asking price of home.

- Property Tax – property tax due within two months of purchase.

- ❯ Rate Lock Fee – fee charged by lender to guarantee a certain interest rate. This is paid usually at the preapproval mortgage process.

- ❯ Recording Fee – fee charged for the recording of deed and other public land records usually by your town or county.

- ❯ Survey Fee – fee charged by a company who checks your property lines.

- ❯ Title Search Fee – a fee charged by a company to research public records like deed records to ensure there are not any liens against the property.

- ❯ Transfer Tax – taxed charged for the transfer of the title from the seller to the buyer.

- ❯ Underwriting Fee – fee charged by the lender for the writing up of your mortgage/loan.

Michelle can expect to pay 2 to 5 percent of the purchase price, and closing costs may vary from region to region of the United States. To reduce these costs, the buyer may ask the seller to cover some of the costs. Another way is to negotiate some of the costs if possible (your lender or attorney can help you figure that out) or if you participate in a first-time homebuyer program, the program may grant you money toward the costs. Also, you may shop around to compare costs, and as a last resort, you can ask the lender to roll costs into your mortgage. However, you may pay a higher fee or interest rate for that option.

After our consultation, Michelle is ready to purchase her new home. She feels confident that she has all the information to make an educated and right decision in the purchase of her new home.

REITS

There are other ways to invest in real estate without actually owning a home. You may invest in an investment vehicle called a REIT which stands for Real Estate Investment Trust. REIT investments act like mutual funds and cover a variety of properties such as apartment buildings, industrial parks, hotels, and offices buildings. It provides the investor the opportunity to share in income produced via rents collected without actually owning and having to manage or finance the property. You can access these investments through your retirement accounts such as your 401k or your brokerage account.

INVESTMENT PROPERTY

Another way to invest in real estate is through investment properties. It can be as simple as purchasing a home and renting it out, to owning a residential building or commercial property. Investment property investing is a great way to build wealth through the generation of income or through capital appreciation. Although purchasing an investment property does a great job in diversifying your portfolio, obtaining financing for it in terms of a mortgage is a bit more complicated in comparison to obtaining one for a primary residence. In the former, it is a bit more stringent. Typically mortgages for investment properties require a higher down payment and may have higher interest rates because lenders find these mortgages to be riskier. These loans may require a down payment of at least 20 to 25 percent, and the interest rate can be as much as 0.5 to 1.0 percent higher. In any case, if you have the means, the investment may be worth it.

NOTES

NOTES

NOTES

NOTES

CHAPTER 8

Retirement Planning

Retirement is like a long vacation in Las Vegas. The goal is to enjoy it the fullest, but not so fully that you run out of money.

—Jonathan Clements

We have a retirement saving problem in this country. Here are some current statistics according to Transamerica Center for Retirement Studies: "The median total household retirement savings for all workers is approximately $50,000 and that 22% of Americans have less than $5,000 in retirement savings with 15% having none at all," and, more importantly, "Seventy percent of millennials are stressed and anxious about saving for retirement with "nearly half of millennials (43 percent) say they fear outliving their savings and investments" (7).

Due to lack of retirement savings, more than half of retirees plan to work in some capacity during formal retirement. Another dilemma is that many individuals have no idea how much to save. Life expectancy after retirement can be as long as fifteen to twenty years. Many do not have that amount in reserve to last them over that time period.

Mary, age fifty, called me for her one-hour consultation. She is a professional executive assistant to an investment banking CEO. She has never married but recently ended a five-year relationship. She recently attended a financial workshop, and she decided to take a very close look at her finances. She realized she had never looked seriously into her finances, and at the age of fifty, knows that she has to get serious about it. She would love to retire at sixty, but she understands that may not be feasible. She makes $90,000 per year and has contributed 5 percent of her income to her 401k with 5 percent employer match. She has accumulated $100,000, but she knows she is way off track in terms of having enough to comfortably retire. Here is where she stands:

Salary: $90,000.

Take-home pay per month: $5,200.

When it comes to determining how much you think you will need for retirement, it really depends on the life-style you desire to live and your estimated life span. Most financial experts believe that you should be able to live off of the equivalent of 80 percent of your final salary. That means theoretically Mary would need $72,000 per year—this is before cost of living increases. There are also a couple of formulas out there to figure out what you may need. A common formula is the **4 percent rule**. This rule states that if you withdraw 4 percent of your portfolio's value in the first year of retirement and thereafter step up the dollar amount withdrawn with inflation, you should be able to have enough to live off of for thirty years. Of course, this is just an estimate, but some critics have issues with this formula because they find that it may be too aggressive. They feel that 4 percent may be too much to withdraw each month because expenses in retirement should be less, but of course, it depends on what you desire to do in retirement. For example, if you love to travel and plan to travel several times per year, then you may have to adjust your yearly allowance. So, how much does Mary need in retirement to withdraw 4 percent each year to get to a yearly income of $72,000 that would last for thirty years with an approximate 5 percent investment return adjusting for inflation of approximately 3 percent per year? She would need $1,800,000 ($72,000/0.04). She currently has $100,000. According to Schwab.com, there are some assumptions that need to be made about the 4 percent rule:

- **It's a rigid rule.** The 4 percent rule assumes you increase your spending every year by the rate of inflation—not on how your portfolio performed—which can be a challenge for some investors. It also assumes you never have years where you spend more or less than the inflation increases. This isn't how most people spend in retirement. Expenses may change from one year to the next, and the amount you spend may change throughout retirement.

- **It applies to a specific portfolio composition.** The rule applies to a hypothetical portfolio invested 50 percent in stocks and 50 percent in bonds. Your actual portfolio composition may differ, and you may change your investments over time during your retirement. We generally suggest that you diversify your portfolio across a wide range of asset classes and types of stocks and bonds and that you reduce your exposure to stocks as you transition through retirement.

❯ **It uses historical market returns.** Analysis by Charles Schwab Investment Advisory, Inc. (CSIA) projects that market returns for stocks and bonds over the next decade are likely to be below historical averages. Using historical market returns to calculate a sustainable withdrawal rate could result in a withdrawal rate that is too high.

❯ **It assumes a thirty-year time horizon.** Depending on your age, thirty years may not be needed or likely. According to Social Security Administration (SSA) estimates, the average remaining life expectancy of people turning sixty-five today is less than thirty years. We believe that retirees should plan for a long retirement. The risk of running out of money is an important risk to manage. But, if you're already retired or older than sixty-five, your planning time horizon may be different. The 4 percent rule, in other words, may not suit your situation.

❯ **It includes a very high level of confidence that your portfolio will last for a thirty-year period.** The rule uses a very high likelihood (close to 100 percent, in historical scenarios) that the portfolio would have lasted for a thirty-year time period. In other words, it assumes that in nearly every scenario the hypothetical portfolio would not have ended with a negative balance. This may sound great in theory, but it means that you have to spend less in retirement to achieve that level of safety. By staying flexible and revisiting your spending rate annually, you may not need to target such a high confidence level. (6)

Another rule is the 25 percent rule, which suggests multiplying your desired annual income by twenty-five. For example, in Mary's case, she would need $1,800,000 ($72,000 (her desired income at retirement) times 25).

So, according to the 4 percent rule and the 25 percent rule, and the desire to live off of 80 percent of her current income, Mary would need $1,800,000 at the time of retirement. This goal, to have $1.8 million at time of retirement at age sixty-five, may be daunting because she is currently at $100,000. If she continues saving at this rate (including employee match), she will have less than $400,000 at a return of 6 percent. She clearly does not have enough. To reach this goal, she would need to invest approximately $5,600 per month. This could be including 401k investment and employee match, but it's a big jump from $375 to $5,600. To reach this goal, she needs to save a significant amount of her take-home pay, well over 50 percent. She can also consider taking on a second job that would allow her to save or devote her second income to retirement savings. She has equity in her home but does not want to consider this in her calculations. Her other option would be to reduce her estimated post-retirement yearly living expenses from $72,000 to a lower amount. For example, some experts state that at a minimum you should have saved up ten times your final salary. Ten times her current salary would be $900,000, not $1.8 million. This dollar amount is more attainable. Mary's living expenses can be lowered if she eliminates all consumer debt, possibly moves to a very low-cost area of the country, or considers working part-time during her retirement years (which many people do). She could also push back her retirement age to sixty-seven instead of sixty-five. This calculation also does not include possible Social Security. Again, Mary wants to be as conservative as possible and save based on the worst possible scenario, i.e., no social security benefits.

These are the various investment vehicles Mary can use for retirement:

Traditional 401(k) or 403(b): For most people, these two plans are the most common. 401k is normally offered to employees of "for profit" companies, and 403b is normally offered to employees of "nonprofit" companies. Contributions are made from your paycheck with

pretax dollars (before tax withholdings). In 2020 and 2021, the maximum amount that can be contributed is $19,500 of your pretax income ($26,000 if you are fifty or older by year's end). This money can be rolled over into a new 401k or a personal IRA account if you leave your job. If you decide to withdraw this money, heavy income tax penalties can occur if you are younger than 59 ½ years old; however, there are some exceptions that you should confirm with your accountant. Once you reach retirement, withdrawals on your distribution are taxed.

Roth 401(k) or 403(b): Contributions are made from your paycheck with ***after-tax dollars (after tax withholdings).*** The maximum contributions are the same as the traditional 401(k) and 403(b). (In 2020 and 2021, the maximum amount that can be contributed is $19,500 of your pretax income; $26,000 if you are fifty or older by year's end). The main difference is that when you make your distributions, that money will be ***tax-free*** since contributions were made with after-tax dollars. This can be significant. Another difference is you must have held the account for five years before you can withdraw the money. The minimum age of distribution without penalty is the same as the traditional one, which is 59 ½ years of age.

457(b) plan: If you are a state and local government employee or work for certain nonprofits, your organization may have a 457-plan account. A 457 plan is a type of tax-deferred plan much like the 401k or 403b with the same contribution limits. And if your company offers both a 401k (403b) AND a 457, you can contribute to both. Also, the catch-up rule occurs earlier than with the 401k and 403b; you can increase your contributions three years prior to "normal retirement age" which is specified in the plan. Also, early distributions—those before age 59 ½—from 457(b) plans are not subject to the ten percent penalty. There are some disadvantages to having a 457 plan. They are:

1. Hardship withdrawals are exceedingly difficult. In order to withdraw money, it has to be for a severe, unforeseen economic hardship.

2. If the organization goes bankrupt, the money in your account can disappear too.

3. Management fees may be higher.

4. Employee matches are rare.

Solo 401(k): A sole proprietor can set up an individual 401(k) and make contributions as both the employee and employer. Per the Internal Revenue Service (IRS), contributions can be made to the plan in both capacities. The maximum that can be contributed in 2020 is $57,000 or $63,500 if you are fifty years or older. The maximum that can be contributed in 2021 is $58,000 or $64,500 if you are fifty years or older.

Traditional IRA: Per IRS guidelines, anyone can contribute up to $6,000 in 2019, 2020, and 2021 to an IRA ($7,000 if you're over fifty) regardless of income. The interest and gains on your IRA are not taxed (tax-deferred) until it is distributed. Prior to 2019, these contributions may be tax deductible if you qualify, and you can contribute until age 70 ½. However, beginning in 2020, there is no age limit for traditional IRA contributions. If you withdraw prior to age 59 ½, you may incur income tax penalties with some exceptions (check with your accountant and IRS guidelines). Prior to 2020, required minimum distributions (RMD) were required at age 70 ½ . However, starting in 2020, the age requirement for RMDs is now age seventy-two. Per the IRS, you are able to contribute to a traditional IRA whether or not you participate in another retirement plan through your employer or business. However, you may not be able to deduct all of your contributions from your income if you or your spouse participates in another retirement plan at work (again confer with your accountant) (8).

Roth IRA: Per IRS guidelines, anyone can contribute up to $6,000 in 2019, 2020, and 2021 to an IRA ($7,000 if you are over fifty) regardless of income. Unlike a traditional IRA, you cannot deduct your contribution against your gross income during tax preparation time. The money you earn accumulates tax-free, and you pay no tax on withdrawals after you reach age 59 ½ (and if you had your account for at least five years). Plus, unlike with regular IRAs, there is no mandatory withdrawal at age seventy-two (meaning you can also leave amounts in your Roth IRA as long as you live). You can withdraw the amount you contributed (but not your earnings) at any time with no penalty or no taxes due, which is not the case with traditional IRAs. There are income guidelines; therefore consult with your accountant or tax advisor to see whether or not you can contribute to a Roth IRA. You can contribute to both a Roth IRA and a traditional IRA, but the limits apply to your total contribution. Also consult with your accountant regarding Roth IRA withdrawals and penalties rules because they vary depending on your age.

NOTES

NOTES

NOTES

CHAPTER 9

What to Do in Special Financial Circumstances

You are braver than you believe, stronger than you seem, and smarter than you think.

—A. A. Milne

WHAT TO DO IN TIMES OF HARDSHIP . . . FINANCIALLY

Honestly, I do not know anyone who has not encountered some financial difficulties at some point during their life. My lean years were during my time in medical school and residency, when I was not working, and my savings started to dwindle. At the time of this writing, in order to combat the spread of the COVID-19 disease, many cities, counties, and states had to go into lockdown and discontinue many services such as travel, dining, hotel, and entertainment. During the COVID-19 pandemic, at one point, 95 percent of all Americans were ordered to stay home. This means many businesses such as restaurants and retail stores had to close or have employees work from home. Only essential businesses such as hospitals, takeout eateries, and grocery stores, for example, could remain open. As a result, many individuals found themselves out of work and furloughed. At one point during the pandemic, eleven million Americans were out of work. A staggering amount! If you find yourself out of a job or unsure of the security of the one you currently hold, these are the steps to undertake:

DON'T PANIC!

Do not panic, breathe, and begin to assess where you stand. Absolutely do not ignore those bills—that is the worst thing you can do because they will not go away. Take a different perspective and a hard look and say, "Okay this is a challenge, a temporary one, I will overcome." Try to have a positive attitude about it, but do not ignore the phone calls or mail. Each late payment will affect your credit and your score. A thirty-day-plus late payment stays on your credit report for at least seven years and can drop your score fifty to sixty points. A bankruptcy can drop your score by 100 points and will stay on your report for ten years.

CALL YOUR CREDITORS

Be proactive and call every one of your creditors the minute issues arise. Explain your situation and work out a payment plan with them. These creditors include your insurance, credit card and mortgage companies, and automobile lenders. Many creditors have hardship programs that can reduce your monthly payment or your interest rate or revise the terms of a loan. Creditors would rather work with you than write off a balance as a loss. This includes student loan debt holders who may be able to apply for a forbearance, which will allow stoppage on payments temporarily.

CONSOLIDATE DEBT

If you are able, transfer balances to a zero-interest credit card and pay off that balance during the specified time period—all your payments will reduce the principal balance. Apply extra income like a bonus, income tax refund, and monies from a second job to the credit balances. This leads me to my next point…

DO NOT ADD MORE DEBT

Once you pay off a balance or you find yourself debt free, do not add more debt. Now, I know that might seem like super common sense, but there are plenty of individuals who find themselves filing for bankruptcy multiple times because they did not change their behavior. Think of your overall financial goals, make plans, and set priorities to achieve those goals.

Some other steps:

- Apply for unemployment if you are furloughed or laid off and start the process as soon as you are laid off.

- Keep priority obligations on track. Priority obligations include mortgage, rent, groceries, prescriptions, and utilities. Again, be proactive and call your mortgage holder or landlord and make arrangements if you're laid off or think you will be.

- Develop an emergency spending budget.

- Stop non-essential spending now, which should be easy to do, because most places like concert halls, movie theaters, and restaurants are closed.

- BEEF UP EMERGENCY FUNDS IF YOU CAN!

- Identify community resources and government assistance programs if available. Community agencies may help with food banks, temporary assistance with utilities, etc.

- Reach out to a nonprofit financial counselor to find ways to eliminate debt and reduce financial obligations.

- Obtain disability insurance if possible.

- Reevaluate investment accounts including 401k, 403b. Meet with an advisor and review goals and risk adversity.

- This is a great time to make a will or trust and to update beneficiaries on your life insurance policy and other benefits. Meet with an attorney to start the process if you have not already.

WHEN YOU ARE FINANCIALLY STABLE – NEXT STEPS

Set your goals and priorities, budget, begin saving and investing, meet with your financial team (accountant, planner, and advisor) regularly, and enjoy financial freedom!

WHAT TO DO IF YOU GET A WINDFALL LIKE AN INHERITANCE OR LOTTERY WIN

You receive a large windfall and inheritance. It was a shock because you were not expecting it. You are thankful because your financial situation has changed for the better. Now that you have gotten over the shock, what is your next step? NOTHING. Do nothing with that money for a couple of months. Park it into a safe money market account, CD, or savings account for six months. During this time, meet with a fee-based financial planner/advisor, attorney, and banker for the sole purpose of mapping out a plan. Make no major decisions or large purchases during this time. Try to ward off eager family and friends who are eager to share in your winnings; if you are able to remain anonymous, choose that option. You have plenty of time to spend that money. During this time, you have to consider the tax implications of receiving a large windfall and insurance considerations such as beneficiaries and asset protection, estate planning, investing, and charitable giving. If you have debt, applying your windfall to eliminate the debt should be considered first.

WHAT TO DO IF YOU OWE THE IRS OR YOUR STATE TAX AUTHORITY

You have to be completely upfront and proactive. Do not let the Internal Revenue Service or your state tax authority come after you. If you owe taxes, decide how you want to satisfy your debt. The IRS can make your life miserable in ways such as paycheck garnishment and liens. There are several ways to satisfy debt:

- Utilize your savings.

- Pay off with a zero balance transfer credit card with the plan to pay off in short period of time (less than two years). Not an ideal option but you may save on interest and penalties.

- Last resort—make payment arrangements with the IRS or state tax authority. Taxes and penalties will apply.

Regardless of what option you choose, choose something, and make plans to satisfy debt.

WHAT TO DO IN THE EVENT OF A DIVORCE

After ten years of marriage and many years of marriage counseling, Kelvin and Joan are considering divorce. They are both thirty-eight years of age and have two kids, ages eight and seven. They are both lawyers and jointly earn $300,000 per year.

Joan came to my office for advice. She knows she needs to take proactive steps with the divorce looming. She is upset and worried about her future and her children's, but she knows that she needs to be ahead of the fray and begin to make plans. Here are my suggestions:

1. Make a budget based on solo income. She is not a stay-at-home mom, so she has a basis to get an estimate of what her monthly revenue and expenses may look like in her new normal. She may want to estimate probable child support and/or spousal support if possible. This leads me to the next step…

2. Seek advice from a divorce attorney to discuss legal ramifications.

3. Seek advice from an estate attorney for estate planning and for a discussion on wills, trust, power of attorney, and living wills.

4. Sit with a certified public accountant to discuss tax strategies.

5. Reevaluate insurance policies, and ensure you have a disability policy and life insurance. Make appropriate changes to beneficiaries if necessary.

6. Prioritize retirement planning and ensure you have an emergency fund.

7. Self-care—take the time to do something for yourself while you are going through these trying times.

NOTES

NOTES

NOTES

CHAPTER 10

Your Financial Team

Alone we can do so little;
together we can do so much.

—Helen Keller

Financial success depends not only on your desire to be financially stable and independent, it is also dependent on your financial team. Your team should include an accountant, financial planner, banker, and attorney. Another member not frequently mentioned is a financial mentor or coach. A mentor or coach can serve as a role model to you and as an accountability partner to not only teach you what they know but also to help keep you on track. Changing habits, especially bad financial habits, is difficult and seeking help in this area may be the difference between success and failure.

NOTES

NOTES

NOTES

NOTES

1. Webb, Hannah. "The Unforeseen Effects of Financial Disparities During the COVID-19 Pandemic." April 14, 2020. www.igrad.com/ articles/the-unforeseen-effects-of-financial-dispari-ties-during-the-covid-19-pandemic.

2. "High School Graduates who Work Full Time had Median Weekly Earnings of $718 in Second Quarter." TED: The Economics Daily. U.S. Bureau of Labor Statistics, July 21, 2017. www.bls.gov/opub/ted/2017/ high-school-graduates-who-work-full-time-had-median-weekly-earnings-of-718-in-second-quarter. htm#:~:text=Median%20weekly%20earnings%20 of%20full,those%20with%20a%20bachelor's%20de-gree.

3. Haughwout, Andrew, Donghoon Lee, Joelle Scal-ly, and Wilbert van der Klaauw. "U.S. Consum-er Debt Payments and Credit Buffers on the Eve of COVID-19." Liberty Street Economics. Federal

Reserve Bank of New York, May 5, 2020. https://libertystreeteconomics.newyorkfed.org/2020/05/us-debt-payments-and-credit-buffers-on-the-eve-of-covid-19.html.

4. "An Introduction to 529 Plans." U.S. Securities Exchange Commission, May 29, 2018. www.sec.gov/reportspubs/investor-publications/investorpubsintro529htm.html.

5. "What is Compound Interest?" Investor.gov. U.S. Securities Exchange Commission. www.investor.gov/additional-resources/information/youth/teachers-classroom-resources/what-compound-interest

6. Williams, Rob and Chris Kawashima. "Beyond the 4% Rule: How Much Can You Spend in Retirement?" Schwab.com, July 17, 2020. www.schwab.com/resource-center/insights/content/beyond-4-rule-how-much-can-you-safely-spend-retirement#:~:text=One%20frequently%20used%20rule%20of,withdraw%20to%20account%20for%20inflation.

7. Christian, Rachel. "50 Essential Retirement Statistics for 2020." Annuity.org, September 29, 2020. www.annuity.org/retirement/retirement-statistics/.

8. "Retirement Topics - IRA Contribution Limits." Internal Revenue Service. United States Government, November 25, 2020. www.irs.gov/retirement-plans/plan-participant-employee/retirement-topics-ira-contribution-limits.

9. "Credit and Your Consumer Rights." Consumer Information. Federal Trade Commission, June 2017. www.consumer.ftc.gov/articles/0070-credit-and-your-consumer-rights.

10. "Free Credit Reports." Consumer Information, Federal Trade Commission, March 2013. www.consumer.ftc.gov/articles/0155-free-credit-reports.

ABOUT THE AUTHOR

As one of the nation's most acclaimed pediatricians and financial experts, Dr. Randi B. Nelson (a.k.a. DrRandiB-MD) is a nationally recognized author, speaker, and consultant. In addition, she is a sought-after media expert regarding children's and young adults' health issues. Due to her fourteen-year career in investment banking, she is also a financial wellness expert.

Dr. Randi earned her BS in Accounting from State University of New York, Buffalo, her MBA from Hofstra University, and her MD from State University of New York, Stony Brook School of Medicine. She completed her pediatric residency at Jacobi Medical Center in the Bronx, New York. Dr. Randi is a published author in the *Chicken Soup for the Soul* series with her short autobiographical story *Following My Heart.*

Dr. Randi currently lives in Brooklyn, New York. To connect, email her at DrRandi@DrRandibmd.com

CREATING DISTINCTIVE BOOKS
WITH INTENTIONAL RESULTS

We're a collaborative group of creative masterminds
with a mission to produce high-quality books to position
you for monumental success in the marketplace.

Our professional team of writers, editors, designers,
and marketing strategists work closely together to ensure
that every detail of your book is a clear representation
of the message in your writing.

Want to know more?
Write to us at info@publishyourgift.com
or call (888) 949-6228

Discover great books, exclusive offers, and more at
www.PublishYourGift.com

Connect with us on social media

@publishyourgift